A
CENSUS OF NEWINGTON
CONNECTICUT

Taken According to Households in 1776

by
JOSIAH WILLARD

Together with some

DOCUMENTS RELATING TO THE EARLY
HISTORY OF THE PARISH

Edited by
EDWIN STANLEY WELLES
Member of the Connecticut Historical Society

HERITAGE BOOKS
2020

HERITAGE BOOKS

AN IMPRINT OF HERITAGE BOOKS, INC.

Books, CDs, and more—Worldwide

For our listing of thousands of titles see our website
at
www.HeritageBooks.com

A Facsimile Reprint
Published 2020 by
HERITAGE BOOKS, INC.
Publishing Division
5810 Ruatan Street
Berwyn Heights, Md. 20740

Originally published:
Frederic B. Hartranft
Hartford, Conn.
1909

International Standard Book Number
Paperbound: 978-0-917890-77-2

A CENSUS OF

NEWINGTON, CONNECTICUT

1776

A
CENSUS OF NEWINGTON
CONNECTICUT

Taken According to Households in 1776

by
JOSIAH WILLARD

Together with some

DOCUMENTS RELATING TO THE EARLY
HISTORY OF THE PARISH

Edited by
EDWIN STANLEY WELLES
Member of the Connecticut Historical Society

Published by
FREDERIC B. HARTRANFT
HARTFORD, CONN.
1909

Facsimile Reprint Edition
1986
By

HERITAGE BOOKS, INC.
3602 Maureen Lane, Bowie, MD 20715
Phone (301)-464-1159

ISBN 0-917890-77-9

Complete Catalog
Listing Several Hundred Titles
on History, Genealogy & Americana
Available on Request

TABLE OF CONTENTS

PREFACE

The story of this parish census is interesting. Its inception really dates back to an act of the memorable Continental Congress. At a session held Tuesday, December 26, 1775, "The Congress took into consideration the report of the Committee on the State of the Treasury, and thereupon came to the following resolutions:

"Whereas an estimate hath lately been formed of the public expence already arisen, and which may accrue in the defence of America, to the 10 day of June next, in pursuance whereof this Congress, on the 29 day of November, resolved that a farther sum of three millions of dollars be emitted in bills of credit,

Resolved, Therefore that the thirteen United Colonies be pledged for the redemption of the bills of credit so directed to be emitted.

That each colony provide ways and means to sink its proportion of the said bills, in such manner as may be most effectual, and best adapted to the condition, circumstances, and equal mode of levying taxes in each colony.

That the proportion or quota of each respective colony be determined according to the number of inhabitants, of all ages, including negroes and mulattoes in each colony.

That it be recommended to the several assemblies, conventions, or councils, or committees of safety of the respective colonies, to ascertain, by the most impartial and effectual means in their power, the number of inhabitants in each respective colony, taking care that the lists be authenticated by the oaths of the several persons who shall be entrusted with this service; and that the said assemblies, conventions, councils, and committees of safety, do respectively lay before this

Congress a return of the number of inhabitants of their respective colonies, as soon as the same shall be procured."[1]

In response to this resolution the General Assembly of Connecticut at its May session, 1776, enacted,

" That the selectmen in the respective towns in this Colony, at or before the first day of September next, shall take and transmit to his Honor the Governor a particular and exact account of all the persons in their respective towns in this Colony, as well negroes or slaves for life as white persons, distinguishing the number of those who are under the age of twenty years from those who are above that age, the sexes, or whether married or single, those in the militia, and all able bodied men who do not belong to the militia, also all those who are now in actual service, thereby to enable his Honor to prepare a compleat answer to a letter lately received from the Hon[ble] John Hancock, Esq[r], President of the Continental Congress[2]; and that this act be forthwith printed, and distributed by the Representatives in the present Assembly[3]; and that the account or whole number of the persons in each town be attested on oath by the selectmen thereof, to have been faithfully and truly made and completed."[4]

---

[1] Journals of the Continental Congress, Washington, 1905, Vol. III, 1775, pp. 457 and 458.

[2] This letter cannot be found. The one sent to the General Court of Massachusetts reads as follows:

" Philadelphia 2[d] Jan[y] 1776

Hon:[ble] Gentlemen

I have the honor to transmit you several Resolutions pass'd in Congress, to which beg leave to refer you — The Money orderd in consequence of the Accounts you were pleased to transmit to your Delegates, sets off this day, of w:[ch] M[r] Cushing is so kind as to take charge. I hope it will arrive safe, and that the conduct of your Delegates in this instance will meet your Approbation —

As I am now called upon to attend public bussiness, I beg leave to refer you to M[r] Cushing for further particulars —

Wishing you the Compliments of the Season I have the honour to be, Gent: Your most obed:[t] Serv:[it]

JOHN HANCOCK President "

Hon. The Assembly

[3] Mr. Bates, the librarian of the Connecticut Historical Society, has called my attention to the fact that the accounts of Ebenezer Watson of Hartford show that he printed for the Colony a " Resolve for numbering the people of this colony," and also " Additions to resolve for numbering " [the people of this colony], by the middle of June, 1776.

[4] Colonial Records of Connecticut, Vol. XV, pp. 312 and 313.

It was in pursuance of this resolution that Josiah Willard (Aug. 9, 1739 — April 1, 1818), a member of one of the oldest and most influential families in Newington, took the census of the parish.

A few years ago, the original manuscript containing the census from which my father, the late Roger Welles, transcribed the copy here printed, was in the possession of Mr. William A. Willard of Hartford, but is now unfortunately missing.

One or two other facts however in regard to taking the census in Connecticut, we do know.

The original resolution presented to the Lower House, with the exception of the precise date and the last clause which were added in the Upper House, was " Submitted by us your Honor's Humble Sev^ts."

" Jed^h Elderkin
  Daniel Sherman
  Marshf^d. Parsons   } Comm^ee
  Oliver Stanley "

Of this Committee Jedidiah Elderkin, Deputy for Windham, was also a Member of the Council of Safety, Daniel Sherman was Deputy for Woodbury, Marshfield Parsons, Deputy for Lyme and Oliver Stanley, Deputy for Wallingford.

The scheme according to which the census should be taken, is outlined in Document 110, Volume IV, entitled Revolutionary War, in the Archives at the State Library, Hartford.

As some may be curious to know what it was, an exact copy is here given: —

	Males under ten Years
	Females under ten Years
M | S	Males between ten & twenty Married or Single
M | S	Females between ten & twenty Married or Single
M | S	Males between twenty & Seventy Married or Single
M | S	females between twenty & Seventy Married or Single
M | S	Males Above Seventy Married or Single
M | S	females Above Seventy Married or Single
	Officers & Soldiers in Malitia Rolls
	Able Bodied Men between 16. & 45 — not in Malitia Rolls
	Men in the Continental Army
	Men Raised for defence of ye Colony & now in ye Colony
	Negro Males under Twenty
	Negro females under Twenty
	Negro Males above Twenty
	Negro females Above Twenty

(Included in ye foregoing Numbers)

On the back of this document are these endorsements:
In the Lower House
This plan accepted and Approved and Ordered that the Numbers of the Inhabitants of this Colony be taken Accordingly

Test TITUS HOSMER Clerk

In the upper House
Concurrd with this addition viz — these words, " included in the foregoing Numbers "— as noted in the pl.

Test GEORGE WYLLYS *Secrety*

Concurred in the Lower House
Test TITUS HOSMER Clerk

How faithfully Josiah Willard performed his task can be seen by turning to his census.

The missing dates supplied by me and printed in italics, are to be found, unless otherwise stated, in the Wethersfield Records of Births, Marriages and Deaths. A few other facts have been inserted which, it is believed, will enhance the value of the census to the genealogist and local historian.

E. S. W.

The Brick House,
Newington Conn.,
August 31, 1908

Our ancestors, by a wise attention to the home government for nearly two hundred years, came to be the best prepared people there were in the world for self-government.— PRESIDENT TAFT at the Norwich Celebration, July 5, 1909.

A CENSUS OF NEWINGTON

August A. D. 1776.

Record of all the persons living in Newington, taken by families or households, in 1776 by Josiah Willard.

		Born
1	Joshua Andrus	Dec. 11 1707
2	Sybil (*Stoddard*) Andrus	Nov. 4 1705
3	Fitch Andrus	Oct. 12 1739
4	William Andrus	May 24 1710
5	Lois (*Whaples, Stephens*) Andrus[1]	
6	Sylvia Andrus	Apr. 17 1762
7	Cynthe Andrus	Oct. 15 1765
8	Rhoda Andrus	Oct. 14 1768
9	Lemuel Andrus	Nov. 15 1771
	Naomi Andrus (added later)	*bapt. Sept. 22, 1782*[2]
10	Mary (*Gillett*) Andrus[3]	Nov. 2 1699
11	Eli Andrus	Jan. 8 1737
12	Clement Andrus	Oct. 31 1739
13	Abel Andrus	May 6 1735
14	Eunice (*Stoddard*) Andrus	[*Aug. 22*] Sept. 1745
	(*according to Andrews Memorial, p. 95*)	
15	Amos Andrus	Mar. 17 1765
16	Ruth Andrus	Oct. 9 1766
17	Jared Andrus	Apr. 10 1769
18	Hannah Andrus	Feb. 1 1774
	Lydia Andrus (added later)	*bapt. May 20, 1781*[4]
19	Sarah (*Welles*) Andrus *widow of Joseph*	Sept. 1716
20	Elias Andrus	Feb. 16 1753
21	Phinehas Andrus	May 26 1712

[1] Lois, widow of Darius Stephens, dau. of Jacob Whaples, who married William Andrus, March 15, 1759, Andrews Memorial, p. 90; and died Sept. 19, 1825, aged 95. Annals of Newington, pp. 107 and 171.

[2] Annals of Newington, p. 97.

[3] Widow of Caleb Andrus, who died Nov. 24, 1775. She died January 1, 1786. See Andrews Memorial, pp. 70 and 71.

[4] Annals of Newington, p. 96.

		Born
22	Lois (*Williams*) Andrus	July 1723
23	Appleton Andrus	Aug. 8 1757
24	Phinehas Andrus	July 19 1763
25	Miles Andrus	May 22 1735
26	Phebe (*Hurlbut*) Andrus[1]	
27	Miles Andrus	July 7 1759
28	Irene Andrus	Jan. 17 1761
29	Phebe Andrus	Apr. 25 1762
30	Jason Andrus	Feb. 21 1768
31	Benajah Andrus	Nov. 13 1769
32	Titus Andrus	*May 2, 1775*[2]
33	Joseph Andrus	Ap. 13 1743
34	Asenath (*Whaples*) Andrus	Mar. 13 1742
35	Ruth Andrus	Jan. 27 1763
36	Mary Andrus	Jan. 8 1770
37	Roxalana Andrus	Dec. 4 1771
38	Elisha Andrus	Oct. 11 1773
39	Bille Andrus	Nov. 16 1775
	Sarah Andrus (added later)	Sept. 13 1777
	Kata Andrus " "	May 1779
	Asenath Andrus[3] " "	
40	Asa Andrus	Apr. *10*, 1746
41	Chloe (*Andrus*) Andrus	Mar. 3 1748
42	Frederic Andrus	July 24 1768
43	Lyman Andrus	July 1 1772
44	Chloe Andrus	Feb. 3 1775
	Asa Andrus (added later)	
45	Sarah Andrus	
46	Silas Andrus	Ap. 23 1750
47	Oliver Atwood	Mar. 1 1716
48	Dorothy (*Curtis*) Atwood	
49	Levi Atwood	May 10 1752
50	John Atwood	Apr. 16 1755
51	Asher Atwood	Dec. 27 1729
52	Mary (*Mitchelson*) Atwood *Died Mar. 27, 1816, aged 88*[4]	
53	Bette Atwood	Feb. 5 1759
54	Mary Atwood	Dec. 12 1762
55	Ezekiel Atwood	Aug. 19 1764

[1] Daughter of Joseph Hurlbut of Goshen. Andrews Memorial, p. 143.

[2] Andrews Memorial, p. 143.

[3] The Wethersfield Records of Births, Marriages and Deaths give the birth of Asenath Andrus as May 22, 1779, and omit the name of Kata from the family record.

[4] Annals of Newington, p. 169. She was from Simsbury.

Born

56	Daniel Atwood	
57	Rev. Mr. Joshua Belden	July 1724
58	Honor (*Goodrich, Whiting*) Belden[1]	Feb. 22, 1731-2
59	Mary Belden	Dec. 9 1755
60	Sarah Belden	Sept. 29 1757
61	Anna Belden	July 6 1759
62	Martha Belden	July 24 1761
63	Octavia Belden	Oct. 27 1763
64	Rhoda Belden	May 29 1766
65	Joshua Belden	Mar. 29 1768
	Hezekiah Belden (added later)	Feb. 17 1778
66	Enos Blakesly	
67	Jonathan Blinn	Oct. 1 1711
68	Sarah Blinn	Oct. 5 1727
69	Sarah Blinn	Jan. 31 1759
70	Jonathan Blinn	Sept. 28 1762
71	Lucy Blinn	Jan. 8 1766
72	James Blinn	Dec. 11 1730
73	Lois (*Wolcott*) Blinn	July 1742
74	Lois Blinn	Mar. 17 1757
75	James Blinn	May 14 1760
76	Elisha Blinn	Mar. 26 1763
77	Unni Blinn	Mar. 25 1765
	Abigail Blinn (added later)	March 1777
	Nancy Blinn " "	Oct. 1778
78	Rhoda Blinn[2]	*Jan. 17, 1756*
79	Israel Bordman	Sept. 18 1721
80	Rebekah (*Meekins*) Bordman *Died Dec. 9, 1814, aged 91*[3]	
81	Elijah Bordman	*Mar. 31, 1752*
82	Samuel Bordman	Jan. 24, 1755
83	Rebekah Bordman	June 3 1759
84	George Bradley	
85	Peletiah Buck	Sept. 2 1698
86	Jemima Buck	Oct. 2 1705
87	Anne Buck	Apr. 26 1747
88	Hannah Butler	*Apr. 12, 1748*
89	Israel Jennings	
90	Lydia Butler	*Apr. 12, 1748*
91	Charles Churchell	*Dec. 31, 1723*[4]

---

[1] Daughter of Hezekiah Goodrich of Wethersfield and widow of Capt. Charles Whiting of Norwich. Annals of Newington, p. 122.

[2] She was the daughter of Mary Hurlbut and " of James Blinn as she saith ": and married Joseph North, June 2, 1777. Annals of Newington, p. 109.

[3] Annals of Newington, p. 169.

[4] The Churchill Family in America, p. 330.

		Born
92	Lydia (*Belden*) Churchell	*Sept. 6, 1725*
93	Charles Churchell	May 3 1755
94	Samuel Churchell	*Apr. 5, 1757*
95	Hannah Churchell	Dec. 27 1758
96	Solomon Churchell	July 29 1764
97	Silas Churchell	Apr. 1769
98	Levi Churchell	May 28 1752
99	Elizabeth (*Hurlbut*) Churchell	*Dec. 28, 1748*
100	Elizabeth Churchell	Jan. 20 1773
101	Lydia Churchell	Nov. 6 1775
	Noble Churchell (added later)	Nov. 11 1778
102	Joseph Churchell	
103	Nathaniel Churchell	
104	Martha Cole *dau. of Phinehas Cole, bapt. Aug. 19, 1750*[1]	
105	John Camp	Dec. 25 1711
106	Penelope (*Deming*) Camp	Nov. 17 1717
107	Joseph Camp	July 1744
108	Anne (*Kellogg*) Camp	Apr. 16 1749
109	Anne Camp	Apr. 8 1773
110	Ellener Camp.	*July 17, 1775*
	Sarah Camp (added later)	June 6 1778
	Joseph Camp " "	*Mar. 26, 1781*
111	James Camp	Nov. 30, 1746
112	Elizabeth (*Kilbourn*) Camp[2]	
113	John Camp	Apr. 6 1770
114	Samuel Camp	Aug. 25 1772
115	Abigail Camp	Oct. 30 1774
	Moses Camp (Added later)	Apr. 15 1777
	Mary Camp " "	*Oct. 14, 1778*
116	Jonathan Curtiss	*Dec. 26, 1714*
117	Hannah Curtiss[3]	Mar. 1720
118	Joseph Curtiss	June 1756
119	Hannah Curtiss	Mar. 15 1758
120	Polly Cooley	
121	Janna Deming	Nov. 2 1718
122	Anna (*Kilbourn*) Deming [*June 20, 1728*] June 1729	
123	Elias Deming	Apr. 11 1752
124	Thomas Deming	Oct. 27 1755
125	Anne Deming	Mar. 5 1758

---

[1] Annals of Newington, p. 88.

[2] Elizabeth Kilbourn, who married (1) James Camp, Dec. 4, 1769; married (2) Zadock Hinsdale, Jan. 28, 1787, and died Feb. 28, 1814. Annals of Newington, pp. 108 and 111, and Hinsdale Genealogy, p. 81.

[3] Widow of Reuben Whaples, who died Oct. 22, 1748. She married Jonathan Curtiss, March 27, 1755. Annals of Newington, pp. 106 and 113, and Wethersfield Land Records, Vol. XIII, p. 15.

		Born
126	Eunice Deming	Apr. 6 1760
127	John Deming	May 6 1762
128	Chloe Deming	Apr. 25 1765
129	Honor Deming	May 4 1767
130	Gad Deming	June 19 1770
131	Levi Deming	Aug. 27 1772
132	Stephen Deming	Aug. 25 1723
133	Hannah (*Goodrich*) Deming	*May 15, 1725*[1]
134	Rosanna Deming	Dec. 3 1750
135	Sylvia Deming	July 5 1759
136	Leonard Deming	Sept. 7 1763
137	Hannah (*Lusk*) Deming[2]	
138	Ephraim Deming	Feb. 25 1761
139	Frederic Deming	May 17 1765
140	Lucretia Deming	Mar. 19 1767
141	Selah Deming	Mar. 6 1769
142	Roger Deming	July 19 1771
143	Francis Deming	Jan. 1739
144	Mary (*Camp*) Deming	Dec. 21 1740
145	Nancy Deming	Dec. 11 1762
146	Robert Deming	Dec. 26 1763
147	Barzilla Deming	Mar. 21 1766
148	Joseph Deming	July 23 1769
149	Mary Deming	Oct. *15*, 1770
150	Jedidiah Deming	Apr. 15 1713
151	Rebekah Deming	*Nov. 10, 1754*[3]
152	Elizur Deming	Feb. 3 1751
153	Lucina (*Francis*) Deming	Apr. 7 1753
154	James Deming	July *29*, 1776
	Anne Deming (Added later)	*Oct. 19, 1780*
155	Ebenezer Dickinson	Dec. 1733
156	Mabel Dickinson	Apr. 25 1737
157	Waitstill Dickinson	July 2 1758
158	Hannah Dickinson	Oct. 9 1761
159	Oren Dickinson	Sept. 20 1766
160	Ebenezer Dickinson	June 11 1771
	Oren Dickinson (added later)	June 10 1779
161	Samuel Davis	
162	Anne Davis	

---

[1] Deming Genealogy, p. 67.

[2] Hannah (Lusk) Deming was the widow of Waitstill Deming, who died March 10, 1776. Deming Genealogy, p. 68.

[3] The correct date of birth, if, as probable, this Rebecca was the daughter of Gamaliel Deming, who married Joseph Curtis, Dec. 15, 1778. Deming Genealogy, p. 71.

		Born
163	Anne Davis	Nov. 10 1767
164	Samuel Davis	Nov. 5 1772
165	Mary Davis	Apr. 6 1775
	Bille Davis (added later)	Jan. 1778
166	William Dunston	
167		
168	Elizabeth Dunston	
169		
170	Lydia Fox	June 1735
171	Sarah Francis *probably widow of Sergt. Thomas*	
		Apr. 1716
172	Josiah Francis	Sept. 18 1722
173	Melliscent (*Stoddard*) Francis	Jan. 29 1729
174	James Francis	Dec. 4 1755
175	Asa Francis	Nov. 8 1757
176	Allein Francis	Oct. 23 1760
177	Roger Francis	Apr. 29 1763
178	Sarah Francis	Apr. 1769
179	Elias Francis	Apr. 30 1748
180	Thankful (*Hunn*) Francis	June 17 1749
181	Rachel Francis	June 18 1772
182	Seth Hun Francis	Nov. 13 1774
	Levi Francis (added later) *probably bapt. Nov. 10, 1776*[1]	
183	Justus Francis	Nov. 8 1750
184	Keturah (*Andrus*) Francis	Nov. *14,* 1752
	Appleton Andrus Francis (added later)	Aug. 9 1778
185	Hezekiah Francis	Mar. 11 1738
186	Deborah Francis[2]	
187	Rosewell Francis	Dec. 27 1762
188	Hosea Francis	Oct. 14 1764
189	Thomas Francis	Aug. 10 1766
190	Selah Francis	Aug. 10 1766
191	Adonijah Francis	*bapt. Aug 9, 1772*[3]
192	Hannah Francis	*bapt. June 12, 1774*[4]
193	Manda Francis	Aug. 31 1769
194	Hezekiah Francis	*bapt. Feb. 16, 1777*[4]
	Adonijah Francis (added later)	June 28, 1778
195	Olive Frazier[5]	Apr. 2 1753
196	Irene Fuller	Nov. 14 1757

[1] Annals of Newington, p. 95.

[2] Said to have been Deborah Blinn. Stiles' Ancient Wethersfield, Vol. II, p. 340.

[3] Annals of Newington, p. 94.

[4] Annals of Newington, p. 95.

[5] Olive, daughter of Charles Frazier, married January 22, 1778, Phineas Kelogg, who was born June 7, 1756. The Kelloggs in the Old World and the New, Vol. I, p. 214.

		Born
197	Justus Francis 2d	*Jan. 25, 1762*[1]
198	Benjamin Goodrich	July 21 1717
199	Sarah (*Dewey*) Goodrich	*Aug. 2, 1712*[2]
200	Rhoda Goodrich	*Mar. 23, 1750*
201	David Goodrich	*Mar. 16, 1757*
202	John Goodrich[3]	*Aug. 21, 1754*
203	Abigail Price	
204	Mary Goodrich	
205	Elizur Goodrich	
206	Hannah Goodrich	
207		
208	John Graham	
209	Hannah (*Hunn*) Graham	*April 2[1],*(?) *1747*

dau. of Samuel Hunn. See Wethersfield Land Records, Vol. XIV, p. 305.

210	Samuel Graham	June 19 1771
211	Clara Graham	June 9 1773
212	Mary Graham	*bapt. June 25, 1775*[4]
	Hannah Graham (added later)	Mar. 30 1777
	Sarah Graham " "	Jan. 7 1779
213	Josiah Griswold	
214	Gideon Hun	Mar. 12 1710
215	Rebecca Hun	Feb. 3 1709
216	Rebecca Hun	Mar. 5 1740
217	Eunice Hun	May 1 1752
218	Enos Hun	Mar. 1 1745
219	Esther (*Smith*) Hun *died June 6, 1817, aged 63*[5]	
220	Elisheba Hun	May 6 1774
	David Hun (added later)	Jan. 29 1779
	Rebecca Hunn " "	*bapt. May 27, 1781*[6]
221	Amos Hurlbut	Apr. 14 1717
222	Sarah (*Latimer*) Hurlbut	May 29 1719
223	Charles Hurlbut	Nov. 4 1707
224	Martha Hurlbut	
225	Jerusha Hurlbut	Apr. 18 1744
226	John Hurlbut	Apr. 10 1751
227	Elias Hurlbut	Feb. 17 1742

[1] Son of Elijah Francis of Berlin. See Francis Family, p. 67.

[2] She was Sarah Dewey, dau. of Daniel and Catherine (Beckley) Dewey. Dewey Genealogy, p. 850.

[3] John Goodrich, 3d, and Abigail Price, married Oct. 1, 1776. Annals of Newington, p. 109.

[4] Annals of Newington, p. 95.

[5] Wethersfield Inscriptions, p. 167.

[6] Annals of Newington, p. 96.

18

		Born
228	Patience (*Blinn*) Hurlbut[1]	
229	Mehitable Hurlbut	June 19 1764
230	Ellener Hurlbut	July 25 1766
231	Martha Hurlbut	Feb. 1 1770
232	Phebe Hurlbut	Jan. 25 1773
233	Absalom Hurlbut	May 29 1775
	Jemima Hurlbut (added later)	June 2 1779
234	Sybil Hurlbut	*Nov. 4, 1705*
235	Fitch Hurlbut	Feb. 27 1726
236	Jemima (*Hunn*) Hurlbut	Aug. 20 1740
237	Lemuel Hurlbut	*Aug. 21, 1750*[2]
238	Tabitha (*Nott*) Hurlbut	*Aug. 21, 1752*[2]
	Hannah Hurlbut (added later)	*April 10, 1777*[2]
	Lemuel Hurlbut " "	*Nov. 10, 1778*[2]
239	Levi Hurlbut	*Mar. 20, 1744*
240	Martha (*Hurlbut*) Hurlbut	Feb. 11 1747
241	Roger Hurlbut	Oct. 1 1767
242	Seth Hurlbut	*Jan. 16, 1775*
243	Martin Kellogg	Aug. 2 1718
244	Mary (*Boardman*) Kellogg	*Sept. 19, 1719*
245	Ellener Kellogg	Mar. 10 1755
246	Jemima Kellogg	*Aug. 23, 1757*[3]
247	Martin Kellogg	July 18 1746
248	Hannah (*Robbins*) Kellogg	*Mar. 10, 1750*
249	Hannah Kellogg	Jan. 17 1774
250	Mary Kellogg	May 26 1776
	Jemima Kellogg (added later)	*Dec. 20, 1778*
	Martin Kellogg " "	*July 24, 1781*
251	Elizabeth (*Russell*) Kellogg	*May 17, 1729*[4]
252	Cynthia Kellogg	May 26,[4] 1764
253	Phineas Kellogg[5]	
254	Eunice Kilborn	Feb. 10, 1719
255	Timothy Kilborn	*Aug. 23, 1723*

[1] She was Patience Blinn and married Elias Hurlbut, April 4, 1764. Annals of Newington, p. 107.

[2] Hurlbut Family, p. 126.

[3] Wethersfield Inscriptions, p. 178.

[4] Elizabeth Russell, daughter of John Russell, Jr., of Wethersfield, married Nov. 9, 1749, Stephen Chester Kellogg, who died Aug. 24, 1767. See The Kelloggs in The Old World and the New, Vol. I, pp. 100 and 101.

[5] Perhaps an error for Joseph, born Feb. 23, 1767. See The Kelloggs in The Old World and the New, Vol. I, p. 101. Phineas, son of Abraham Kellogg of New Hartford, born June 7, 1756, married Olive Frazier of Newington, January 22, 1778. See footnote 5, page 16.

		Born	
256	Prudence (*Deming*) Kilborn[1]		
257	Seth Kilborn	Oct. 27 1754	
258	Happy Kilborn	Aug. 25 1757	
259	Simon Kilborn	Nov. 23 1759	
260	Abigail Kilborn	Sept. 16 1764	
261	Timothy Kilborn Jun[r]	[*May 9*] May 4 1752	
262	Mary (*Deming*) Kilborn[2]		
263			
264	Henry Kirkham	Aug. 30 1728	
265	Mary (*Hurlbut*) Kirkham	Oct. 10 1734	
266	Samuel Kirkham	Mar. 14 1759	
267	John Kirkham	Nov. 5 1760	
268	Eunice Kirkham	May 1764	
269	Abigail Kirkham	Mar. 1 1766	
270	Sarah Kirkham	Feb. 1770	
271	Samuel Landres[3]		
272	Sarah Landres		
273	Samuel Landres	Mar. 30 1765	
274	Sarah Landres	*Aug 3, 1766*	
275	Vannaras Landres	[*June 6, 1771*] July 7 1770	
276	Lemuel Landres	*June 6, 1773*	
277	Hannah Landres	*Nov. 12, 1775*	
278	Luther Latimer	[*Oct. 17*] Oct. 6 1744	
279	Dorothy (*Smith*) Latimer	Dec. 8 1744	
280	Uzziel Latimer	Nov. 1 1769	
281	Esther Latimer	Mar. 17 1772	
282	Olive Latimer	Mar. 1776	
283	Lois Latimer	*May 8, 1750*	
284	Sarah Latimer	*April 12, 1754*	
	Benjamin Landres[4]	Apr. *28*, 1768	
285	David Lowrey	*July 23, 1740*[5]	
286	Lucy (*Cole*) Lowrey	bapt. *Dec. 25, 1748*[6]	
287	Lucy Lowrey	July 26 1771	
	Mary Lowrey (added later)	Dec. 1 1778	
288	John Lusk	May 5 1703	
289	Jane Lusk	Dec. 25 1708	

[1] She was the daughter of Josiah Deming and married Timothy Kilbourn, Aug. 15, 1751. Deming Genealogy, p. 33.

[2] She was Mary Deming and married Timothy Kilbourn, Jr., Jan. 5, 1775. Annals of Newington, p. 109.

[3] Samuel Landers and Lemuel Whittlesey were survivors of the fearful Havana Expedition of 1762, serving in the company of Capt. John Patterson of Farmington. See Stiles' Ancient Wethersfield, Vol. I, pp. 412 and 413.

[4] He was the third child of the foregoing Samuel and Sarah Landers.

[5] Timlow's Sketches of Southington Genealogies, p. 166.

[6] She was Lucy Cole, daughter of Phinehas Cole, and died Feb. 2, 1826, aged 77. See Annals of Newington, pp. 88, 108, and Wethersfield Inscriptions, p. 182.

Born

290	James Lusk	Apr. 17 1746
291	Abigail (*Belden*) Lusk	Aug. 10 1753
	Love (*Graham*) Lusk (added later)	*Oct. 1, 1753*[1]
	Abigail Belden Lusk " "	*July 27, 1781*
292	Mary Lusk[2]	
293	Elijah Lusk	*Dec. 15, 1754*
294	Levi Lusk	bapt. *April 3, 1757*[3]
295	Morris	
296		
297	Abisha Marks	
298	*Rhoda (Latimer) Marks*	*Oct. 25, 1746*
	if as likely, she was the daughter of John and Anna (Grimes) Latimer	
299	Asahel Marks	June 15 1771
	Bildad Marks (added later)	Sept. 2 1777
300	Jedidiah Mills	
301	Sarah (*Andrus*) Mills	Feb. 1756[4]
302	Betsey Mills	Sept. 20 1776
	Sally Mills (added later)	Feb. 21 1778
	Julia Mills " "	Aug. 31 1779
303	Zebulon Mygatt[5]	
304	Samuel Richards	Oct. 1727
305	Lydia Richards	Apr. 22 1725
306	William Richards	Oct. 9 1755
307	Pelatiah Richards	Sept. 5 1759
308	Lucretia Richards	Jan. 4 1762
309	Seth Richards	Oct. 5 1764
310	Selah Richards	Sept. 17 1767
311	Joseph Richards	Oct. 1740
312	*Mary (Kelsey) Richards*	*May 12, 1745*[6]
313	Thomas Richards	Apr. 16 1765
314	Joseph Richards	June 14 1767
315	Oliver Richards	July 8 1769
316	Janna Richards	
317	Unni Robbins	*Feb. 9, 1741-2*
318	Mary (*Kellogg*) Robbins	Apr. 18 1743

---

[1] Suffield Record of Births, Marriages and Deaths, Vol. I, p. 122. Love Graham of Suffield became the second wife of James Lusk.

[2] Mary Lusk was admitted to full communion in the Newington Church, July 1, 1770. Annals of Newington, p. 84.

[3] Annals of Newington, p. 90.

[4] The Wethersfield Records give the birth of Sarah, daughter of Joseph Andrus, who married June 6, 1776, Jedidiah Mills, as Jan. 12, 1756.

[5] Zebulon Mygatt, son of Zebulon of East Hartford, died in Wethersfield, April 8, 1783.

[6] Daughter of Enoch and Mary Kelsey of Berlin. Hartford Probate Files.

		Born
319	Unni Robbins	Nov. 29 1765
320	Prudence Robbins	Jan. 23 1767
321	Martin Robbins	Dec. 30 1770
322	Abigail Robbins	Apr. 18 1775
323	David Russel	*Aug. 29, 1726* [1]
324	Thankful Seymour	Mar. 1712
325	Elias Seymour	Apr. 28 1746
326	Elizabeth (*Wolcott*) Seymour	Aug. 12 1746
327	Jerusha Seymour	Mar. 24 1770
328	David Seymour	May 24 1772
329	Nancy Seymour	Apr. 17 1774
330	Elizabeth Seymour	Sept. 19 1775
	Theodore Seymour (added later)	June 22 1778
	Eunice Seymour " "	*Nov. 24, 1780*
331	Abel Seymour	Feb. 13 1741
332	George Seymour	July 16 1742
333	Ashbel Seymour	Jan. 25 1748
334	Thankful Seymour	Apr. 5 1750
335	Lois Seymour	Oct. 10 1754
336	Luscinda Smith	
337	Joseph Steel	*Sept. 1747 or 8* [2]
338	Olive (*Churchill*) Steel [3]	
339	John Squier	*Died Feb. 8, 1813, aged 75* [4]
340	Rozette (*Blinn, Kirkham*) Squier [5]	
341	Lois Squier	Dec. 29 1761
342	Rozetta Squier [6]	May 1769
343	John Squier	Dec. *14*, 1770
344	Lucy Squier	1773
345	Rhoda Squier	
346	Elisha Stoddard	Aug. 19 1736
347	Dorothy (*Willard*) Stoddard	Sept. 26 1741
	Chloe Stoddard (added later)	Apr. 16 1777
	Elisha Stoddard " "	Sept. 10 1779
	Simeon Stoddard " "	Sept. 12 1782

[1] If, as probable, he was the son of John Russell of Wethersfield. David Russell died in Newington, Jan. 4, 1806, aged 80. Annals of Newington, p. 167. "Nouember ye 20 A D 1764" "Then Came David Rusel to Liue to my House" Entry in an old account book belonging to Gideon Hunn, p. 320.

[2] Son of James and Mercy (Cowles) Steele. Steele Family, p. 25.

[3] Daughter of Giles Churchill. See The Churchill Family, p. 335. She married Joseph Steele, Oct. 27, 1774. Annals of Newington, p. 109.

[4] Annals of Newington, p. 168.

[5] Rosetta Blinn was widow of Nathaniel Kirkham, who died June 26, 1759, at Fort Edward, N. Y. Annals of Newington, p. 114.

[6] Her birth should be May 7, 1768, according to the Wethersfield Records. She married Justus Wolcott, Dec. 12, 1785. Annals of Newington, p. 111.

		Born	
348	Eli Stoddard	Feb.	1739
349	Abigail (*Atwood*) Stoddard	Aug. 28	1747
350	Levi Stoddard	Apr. 9	1771
351	Roxalana Stoddard	Dec. 9	1772
352	Mary Stoddard	Aug. 9	1775
353	Benjamin Stoddard[1]	[*Feb. 2, 1743*] Feb. 2	1742
354	Rhoda Stoddard[1]	[*Oct. 30*] Oct. 31	1754
355	Solomon Stoddard *Died Mar. 18, 1797, in his 67th year*[2]		
356	Anne (*Andrus*) Stoddard		
357	Anne Stoddard	Jan. 11	1760
358	Jonathan Stoddard	Jan. *18,*	1738
359	Sabara (*Andrus*) Stoddard	July 28	1739
360	Anne Stoddard	June 29	1763
361	Sabara Stoddard	July 27	1765
362	Jennet Stoddard	Aug. 31	1767
363	Honor Stoddard	July 16	1770
364	Jonathan Stoddard	[*July 24, 1773*]	1772
365	Olive Stoddard	June 3	1775
366	Enoch Stoddard	Jan. 10	1746
367	Dinah (*Fuller*) Stoddard	Aug.	1749
368	Jehiel Stoddard	Oct.	1769
369	Abigail Stoddard	Feb. *10,*	1776
370	Joseph Stoddard	Aug 21	1747
371	Mary (*Fuller*) Stoddard	Jan. 29	1748
372	Joseph Stoddard	Dec. *23,*	1768
373	Zebulon Stoddard	Aug. *19,*	1770
374	Jesse Stoddard	July *29,*	1772
375	Mary Stoddard	*July 10, 1774*	
	Percy Stoddard (added later) [*Dec. 10, 1778*] Nov. *1778*		
	Candace Stoddard " " *bapt. July 8, 1781*[3]		
376	David Stoddard	Sept. 23	1749
377	Hannah Whaples	Apr. 30	1703
378	Ephraim Whaples		
379	Elizabeth (*Baxter*) Whaples	*Mar. 23, 1707-8*	
380	Huldah Whaples	Sept. 25	1733
381	Ephraim Whaples	Apr. 22	1736
382	Elisha Whaples	Sept. 8	1737

---

[1] Children of Thomas and Mary (Camp) Stoddard. Rhoda Stoddard married Levi Curtis, Jan. 4, 1779, and removed to Lenox, Mass. Stiles' Ancient Wethersfield, Vol. II, p. 686, and Annals of Newington, p. 110.

[2] Wethersfield Inscriptions, p. 175.

[3] Annals of Newington, p. 96.

		Born
383	Daniel Warner	
384	Edward Weaver	
385		
386	Hannah Weaver	Feb. 20 1767
387	Mary Weaver	Sept. 9 1769
388	Eli Whaples	Mar. 1739
389	*Elizabeth (Foster) Whaples*	*June 26, 1739*[1]
390	Sarah Whaples	Mar. 25 1765
391	Reuben Whaples	Feb. 28 1768
392	Honour Whaples	Jan. 14, 1770
393	Elisha Whaples	Feb. 12, 1772
394	Phebe Whaples	May 9 1774
395	Abigail Whaples	
	Samuel Whaples (added later)	July 28 1780
396	Robert Welles Cap't.	Sept. 7 1710
397	Abigail (*Burnham*) Welles	Sept. 1713
398	Sarah Welles	Jan. 22 1738
399	Abigail Welles	Apr. 6 1749
400	Appleton Welles	June 16 1753
401	Rhoda Welles	July 29 1756
402	Robert Welles Jun[r]	Feb. 17 1740
403	Abigail (*Hurlbut*) Welles	June 16 1741
404	Robert Welles	Sept. 27 1761
405	Abigail Welles	Jan. 5 1764
406	Absalom Welles	Mar. 14 1766
407	Hannah Welles	*bapt. June 4, 1769*[2]
408	William Welles	Jan. 14 1707
409	Martha Welles	Oct. 27 1749
410	Levi Welles	July 10 1765
411	Elijah Welles	Oct. 26 1744
412	Sarah (*Kellogg*) Welles	Dec. 18 1750
413	Chester Welles	May 16 1775
	Sarah Welles (added later)	Sept. 9 1777
	Alma Welles " "	*Aug. 29, 1780*
414	James Welles	Feb. 10 1748
415	Lucy(*Wells*)Welles *Died Sept. 13, 1783, in her 38th year*[3]	
416	James Welles	Sept. 6 1772
417	Lucy Welles	*Sept. 29, 1774*
418	Clara Welles	*Feb. 8, 1777*

[1] He married March 7, 1765, Elizabeth, dau. of John and Phebe (Cornwell) Foster of Middletown. First Congregational Church Records of Middletown. For date of birth, see Middletown Records of Births, Marriages and Deaths, Vol. I, p. 85.

[2] Annals of Newington, p. 94.

[3] Wethersfield Inscriptions, p. 169.

Born

	Austin Welles (added later) [*Dec. 23, 1778*] Nov. 23 1778	
	Beulah Welles " "	*Oct. 29, 1780*
419	Lemuel Whittlesey	May 16 1740
420	Hannah (*Welles*) Whittlesey	Apr. 22 1742
421	Hannah Whittlesey	June 8 1765
424	Lemuel Whittlesey	July 3, 1772[1]
423	Dorothy Whittlesey	Mar. 17 1770
424	Lemuel Whittlesey	July 3, 1772[1]
425	Chauncey Whittlesey	Oct. 14, 1777[1]
426	Elizabeth Willard *probably Elizabeth (Filer)*	
	widow of Deacon Josiah	July 2 169-
427	Daniel Willard	July 31 1710
428	Dorothy (*Deming*) Willard	Oct. 21 1716
429	Josiah Willard	Aug. 9 1739
430	Honour Willard	Nov. 5 1746
431	Hannah Willard	Dec. 21 1748
432	William Willard	Nov. 23 1750
433	Daniel Willard	Apr. 7 1753
434	Lydia Willard	May 25 1757
435	Ezekiel Winchell	*Feb. 26, 1758*[2]
436	David Woolcott	Mar. 3 1710
437	Abigail (*Loomis*) Woolcott	Mar. 15 1709
438	Eunice Woolcott	May 26 1748
439	David Woolcott	Aug. 26 1744
440	Hannah (*Munsell*) Woolcott	
441	Hannah Woolcott	Jan. 4 1770
442	Lydia Woolcott	Jan. 6 1772
443	Elizabeth Woolcott	Feb. 1 1774
444	David Woolcott	Jan. 1 1776
445	George Wolcott	[*Jan. 18, 1747*][3] Jan. 1748
446	Elizabeth (*Nott*) Wolcott	[*Sept. 29, 1750*] Oct. 1751
447	George Wolcott	Aug. 16 1774
448	William Wolcott	Apr. 24 1776
	Betsey Wolcott (added later)	Apr. 18 1780
	Sally Wolcott " "	June 20 1782
449	Josiah Wolcott	June 21 1771
450	Sion Wentworth[4]	1754

---

[1] Whittlesey Genealogy, p. 70. Chauncey Whittlesey removed to Lenox, Mass.

[2] If, as probable, he was the son of Dan and Lois (Curtiss) Winchell of Farmington. See Winchell Genealogy, p. 52.

[3] The Wolcott Memorial, p. 127.

[4] Sion Wenthworth, b. ———, 1754, d. April 18, 1823; m. (1) Anna Stoddard, b. Jan. 11, 1760, d. Aug. 2, 1780; (2) May 11, 1789, Rebecca, dau. of Israel and Rebecca (Meekins) Boardman, b. June 3, 1759; d. March 21, 1814. See Boardman Genealogy, p. 670.

		Born
451	Caleb Wolcott	*Dec. 19, 1728*[1]
452	Jerusha (*Price*) Wolcott[2]	
453	Eunice Wolcott	*bapt. Feb. 23, 1755*[3]
454	Elizur Wolcott	May 12 1754
455	Esther (*Andrus*) Wright *widow of Thomas*	
	Wright	*Died Dec. 10, 1811, aged 79*[4]
456	John Wright	Jan. 13 1762
457	Michael Wright	Jan. 19 1765
458	Sarah Wright	Oct. 30, 1767
459	Esther Wright	Apr. 1771
460	Lydia Wright	May 1773

Colored Servants.

461 Guinea *Belonged to Deacon Josiah Willard*
    Annals of Newington, p. 145
462 Prince*
463 Step "*Negro of Lieut. [Martin] Kellogg*"
    Ibid, p. 95
464 Pomp *Owned by Deacon John Camp*
    Ibid, p. 145
465 Mingo   Dec. 26 1763
466 Katern *Belonged to Lieut. Martin Kellogg*
467 Pegg *Daughter of Step and Katern bapt. May 2, 1773*
    Ibid, pp. 95 and 145

    Recapitulation — Whites   460
                Colored   7

          Total = 467.

Families formed or come into the Society since Aug. 1776.

James Mitchell	*Mar. 2, 1732-3*
Hannah (*Warner*) Mitchell	*Oct 3, 1744*
James Mitchell Jun[r]	Jan. 25, 1774
William Mitchell	[*July 28*] July 30 1779
Pelatiah Haydon	June 1768
Lemuel Churchell	Mar. 14 1766
Martha Churchell	Oct. 1769

---

[1] The Wolcott Memorial, p. 127.

[2] She was from Glastonbury.

[3] Annals of Newington, p. 90.

[4] Wethersfield Inscriptions, p. 155.

* Stephen Kellogg deeds land to Prince, negro servant, to Mr. Phinehas Andrus, Dec. 31, 1759, at a place called the Half Moon in the Society of Newington. Wethersfield Land Records, Vol. XI, p. 112.

	Born.
Ethan Lusk	Oct. 2 1770
Ezekiel Deming	Apr. 1763
Samuel Churchell	*April 5, 1757* [1]
Mercy (*Boardman*) Churchell	*Aug. 2, 1757* [1]
Chisleu Churchell	*Dec. 4, 1779* [1]
Joseph Churchell	*Died April 26, 1812, aged 62*
Rhoda (*Goodrich*) Churchell	*Mar. 23, 1750*
Nathaniel Churchell	
Eunice Churchell	
Joseph Curtiss	June 1756
Rebecca (*Deming*) Curtiss	*Nov. 10, 1754* [2]
Elias Deming	*April 11, 1752*
Martha (*Welles*) Deming	*Oct. 27, 1749*
John Hurlbut	Apr. 10 1751
Phebe Hurlbut [3]	
Lucy Hurlbut	Jan. 23 1778
Mary Hurlbut	Jan. 29 1782
Jedidiah Smith	
Elizabeth (*Kellogg*) Smith	
Benajah Bordman	*May 14, 1749*
Martha (*Churchill*) Bordman	*Oct. 5, 1751*
Mekins Bordman	*May 17, 1773* [4]
Edward Howard [5]	July 6 1763
Amos Buck	
Abigail (*Stoddard*) Buck	
Dorothy Buck	
Ashbel Seymour	*Jan. 25, 1748*
Abigail (*Welles*) Seymour	*April 6, 1749*
Ashbel Seymour	Dec. 6 1777
Erastus Seymour	July 2 1779
Elias Deming	*April 11, 1752*
Martha (*Welles*) Deming	*Oct. 27, 1749*
Enos Deming	Aug. 20 1779
William Deming	*Oct. 13, 1782*

---

[1] Stiles' Ancient Wethersfield, Vol. II, p. 226.

[2] Deming Genealogy, p. 71.

[3] Evidently an error. John Hurlburt married, Jan. 12, 1778, *Judith* Horner, sister of Phebe Horner, who was born April 28, 1757. Annals of Newington, p. 110.

[4] Boardman Genealogy, p. 672.

[5] He married Anne Stoddard, Nov. 13, 1783. Annals of Newington, p. 111.

Samuel Pratt   Born.
Hannah (*Wolcott*) Pratt
Huldah Pratt   Apr. 14 1779
Lydia Pratt   [*Jan. 18*] Jan. 13 1780

PRIVATE RECORD OF DEATHS 1784-1795

The "Annals of Newington" show that the deaths entered on the records of the Congregational Church there, are missing from August 31, 1772, to November 23, 1804.

A private record of deaths during that interval in the possession of M. Lewis Stoddard of Newington, is hereunder given: it is unfortunate that the list is so meagre: —

Seth Kilborn's wife died Feb. 22, 1784[1]
Penelope Camp died April 15, 1784
Jonathan Curtis died June 5, 1784
Eunice Andrus died Jan'y 23, 1785
Mary Francis died the night after the 4th of March, 1785
Sybil Andrus died May 30, 1785
Appleton Wells died July 29, 1785
Gideon Hun died August 29, 1785
Oliver Atwood died Sept. 26, 1785
Lemuel Whittlesey Ju[r] died Oct. 8, 1785
Prudence Kilburn died Oct. 21, 1785
Widdow Mary Andrus died Jan'y 1, 1786
Obediah Smith died Jan'y 28 or 29, 1786
Capt. Robert Wells died Feb. 3, 1786
Dea. Joshua Andrus died April 25, 1786.
Zebulon Goodrich died April 6, 1787
Charles Holabud died June 14, 1787
Jane Lusk died the night after the 5th of February, 1789
Rachel Coslet died the night after the 7th of April, 1790
Stephen Deming died April 24, 1790
Widdow Sarah Francis died May 19, 1790
Elisha Stoddard died July 2, 1790
George Woolcut's wife died April 18, 1795
Abigail Woolcut died April 20, 1795

MEMORANDA RELATING TO NEWINGTON 1727-1787

The following memoranda were jotted down by Daniel Willard (July 31, 1710 — June 1, 1800), and are copied from the original manuscript in the possession of Dr. De Forest Willard of Philadelphia.

July 2nd. 1741 There was atached our muster role for to be ready at one hour's warning by Name as foloweth

---

[1] She was Lois, daughter of James and Lois (Wolcott) Blinn, born March 17, 1757, and married Seth Kilbourn, April 19, 1781. See page 13 and Annals of Newington, p. 110.

Ensign Robert Wells

Sar[nt] Caleb Andrus	Daniel Willard	Abraham Waren
Sar[nt] Samuel Churchill	Nathanel Churchill	Elisha Deming
Drumer David Wright	William Andrus	Janna Deming
Cor[pl] Jonathan Whapls	Judah Wright	Benjamin Goodrich
Corporal Zebulin Robins	Henry Kirkham	Jonathan Blin
Samuel Hun	Joseph Andrus	Martain Kellogg
Jonathan Denorah	Jedidiah Atwod	David Colman
Thomas Stodor	Steadman Younge	Thomas Robins
Zebulin Stodor	Elijah Andrus	Charls Holebut
		Josiah Whitellsey

In August 1739 was the war proclaimed betwen England and Spain

November ye 9 1738 I married to my wife Dorothy

upon august 14 1739 my wife taken sick of the intermiting fever for wich I pray god to restore her again to health

my son Josiah Born upon august ye 9: 1739 about three of the Clock in the afternoon

September 9 1787 Died my Beloved Wife in ye 71 year of Her Age

September 4 1776 Died William Willard at East Chester near New York aged 25 years 9 months and 12 days.

October 21 1740 Died my Negro boy called Bristo aged nine year

April 29 1741 Died my sister Mary Griswould[1]

September 26 1741 Was born my daughter Dorrothy

September 20 1742 Died Jabez Whetelsey junior

1732-1733 John Willard, living in Newington;
Ephraim Whaples;
Mr. Beckus.

1727 John Willard,
Simon Willard deceased, Josiah Willard administrator;
Doc. Joseph Andrus;

1727 Josiah Willard;

Nov. 14th. 1742, died Ephraim Deming, father of Mrs. Willard.

1743, died Elizabeth Buck, July 20th.

March 15th. 1744, Chloe [Willard] born ————

1745, War was proclaimed between France and England.

May 2d. 1745, Stephen Deming enlisted for war, Cape Breton

Feb. 2nd. 1746, died, the Rev. Mr. Simon Beckus, pastor of this church at Cape Breton;

Feb. 4th. 1747, died Captain John Camp;

---

[1] Wife of Jonathan Griswold.

Nov. 5th. 1746, Honour [Willard] born ———
Nov. 11th. 1747, Rev. Mr. Joshua Belding, ordained;
Sept. 2nd. 1748, died [Elizabeth] child of Josiah Wright;
Sept. 5th. 1748, died Amos Andrus;
Sept. 15th. 1748, died Hannah Andrus;
Oct. 22nd. 1748, died Ruben W[h]aples;
Dec. 21st. 1748, born Hannah Willard;
Nov. 23rd, 1750, born William Willard;
Dec. 2nd, 1750, died James Patterson;
July 10th. 1752 died [Prudence] wife of Mr. Josiah Deming;
Apr. 7th. 1753, born Daniel Willard about one-half past six
  o'clock in the afternoon.
May 25th. 1757, born Lydia Willard;
May 31st. 1759, died, Mary Willard;
March 30th. 1763, died Chloe Willard;
March 30th. 1766, died Ephraim Willard, my brother;
1739, living in Newington, Samuel Hun;
                              Daniel Hooker;
1735, living in Newington, David Curtis,
1741.   "   "   John Welles;
1739   "   "   Martin Kellog;
1741   "   "   John Camp;
1740   "   "   Elisha Williams.

*A CATALOGUE OF THE CHILDREN THAT CAME TO ME TO SCHOOL AT THE SOUTH SCHOOL IN NEWINGTON IN DECEMBER 1766.

Levi Churchel
Charles Churchel
Samuel Churchel
Hannah Churchel
Elias Deming
Daniel Deming
Thomas Deming
Anne Deming
Eunice Deming
John Deming

Sarah Deming
Martin Deming
Chloe Kirkum
Samuel Kirkum
John Kirkum
Lois Squire
Elizur Woolcot
Abijah Wright
Asa Wright

*A CATALOGUE OF THE CHILDREN THAT CAME TO THE NORTH SCHOOL IN NEWINGTON IN THE WINTER OF THE YEAR 1768.

Elias Andrus
Silas Andrus
Appleton Andrus

Phinehas Andrus
Sylvia Andrus
John Atwood

* From a manuscript in the possession of Dr. De Forest Willard of Philadelphia.

Hezekiah Atwood
Enos Blakesley
Samuel Boardman
Samuel Buck
Charles Churchell
Samuel Churchell
Joseph Curtiss
Miles Curtiss
John Chambers
Titus Deming
Wait Dickinson
Hannah Dickinson
James Francis
Asa Francis
Allein Francis
Roger Francis
Rosewell Francis
Gad Fullar
Eli Hurlbut

Chester Kellogg
Stephen Kellogg
Simeon Kellogg
William Richards
Peletiah Richards
Lucretia Richards
Seth Richards
Samuel Stoddard
Esther Stoddard
Mabel Stoddard
Elizabth Stoddard
Anne Stoddard
Simon Welles
Appleton Welles
Robert Welles
Daniel Willard
David Webster
James, Negro.

The following names not on the above list appear in the "Catalogue" of those attending the North School in the winter of 1769: —

Anne Andrus
Johnson Andrus
Miles Andrus
Pamela Andrus

Betty Atwood
Ezekiel Atwood
Mary Atwood
Hosea Francis

---

*A MINISTER AND SOCIETY RATE FOR THE YEAR 1771.

Made by us this 21 day of Feb. 1772.

Gideon Hun
Charles Churchell }Committee
Elisha Stoddard

Andrus Caleb
Andrus Joshua D^{n}
Andrus Joseph
Andrus Phinehas
Andrus William
Andrus Elijah

Andrus Miles
Andrus Asa
Andrus Joseph J^{r}
Atwood Oliver
Atwood Asher
Andrus Abel

---

* Original in the possession of Dr. De Forest Willard of Philadelphia.

Andrus Eli
Andrus Clement
Buck Peletiah
Blin Jonathan
Blin James
Boardman Israel
Boardman Sherman
Churchel Charles Capt
Camp John D^n
Camp Joseph
Curtis Jonathan
Churchel Joseph
Deming Janna
Deming Jedidiah
Deming Stephen
Deming Waitstil
Deming Gamaliel
Deming Francis
Dickinson Ebenezer
Davis Samuel
Francis Thomas
Francis Josiah
Francis Elias
Francis Hezekiah
Goodrich Benjamin
Goodrich Ebenezer
Hurlbut Charles
Hurlbut Joseph
Hurlbut Fitch
Hurlbut Amos
Hurlbut Christopher
Hurlbut Levi
Hurlbut Elias
Hun Gideon
Kellogg Martin
Kellogg Elizabeth
Kilborn Timothy
Kirkum Henry
Kilborn Eunice
Lusk John
Lusk James
Lowrey David
Latimer Luther
Lee Josiah D^n
Lee Stephen
Robbins Uni

Seymour Bavil & Ashbel
Stoddard Thomas
Stoddard Solomon
Stoddard Jonathan
Stoddard Eli
Stoddard Enock
Stoddard Joseph
Stoddard David
Seymour Elias
Squire John
Stedman Elisha
Welles Robert Capt
Welles William
Welles Robert jr
Wolcott David
Wolcott George
Wolcott Caleb
Wolcott George jr
Whaples Ephriam
Whaples Ephraim junr
Whaples Elisha
Whaples Daniel
Whaples Eli
Whitelsey Lemuel
Wright Thomas
Willard Daniel
Willard Elizabeth
Webster Samuel
Webster Medad
Andrus Epaphras
Andrus Fitch
Andrus Samuel
Atwood Hezekiah
Boardman Benajah
Grayham John
Richards Samuel D^r
Richards Joseph
Kelsey John
Kilborn Eunice jr
Judd James
Steel James junr
Tryon Aaron
Catlin Mary
Holtom Abigail
Merrel Mary
Goodrich Zebelon

Goodrich Zebelon junr

In the old Society
Chester John Col.
Dickinson Thomas
Deming Elisha
Francis Robert
[110]Mitchel James
Standish Hannah
Standish James
Welles Thomas Cap[t]
Welles Solomon Esq
Welles Hezekiah
Wolcott Samuel
Goodrich David

In the Beckleys
part
Andrus Daniel

Deming Jacob
Celsey Charles
[122]Kelsey Enock
Steel Samuel

Sum total 5788-2-6

Four folds

White Thomas
Hooker Elijah
Waters Benjamin
Standish Hannah
Standish James
Crane Lydia
Whitelsey Lemuel
Hunn Gideon

Total — 317-4-0

INDEX

3

35

36

Francis, Adonijah, 16
Allein, 16, 30
Amanda, (Manda), 16
Appleton Andrus, 16
Asa, 16, 30
Deborah, Mrs. Hezekiah, 16
Elias, 16, 31
Hannah, 16
Hezekiah, 16, 31
Hezekiah, Jr., 16
Hosea, 16, 30
James, 16, 30
Josiah, 16, 31
Justus, 16
Justus, 2d, 17
Keturah (Andrus), Mrs. Justus, 16
Levi, 16
Lucina, 15
Mary, 27
Milliscent (Stoddard), Mrs. Josiah, 16
Rachel, 16
Robert, 32
Roger, 16, 30
Rosewell, 16, 30
Sarah, 16
Sarah, widow of Thomas, 16, 27
Selah, 16
Seth Hunn, 16
Thankful (Hunn), Mrs. Elias, 16
Thomas, 16, 31

Frazier, Olive, 16

Fuller, Dinah, 22
Gad, 30
Irene, 16
Mary, 22

G
Gillett, Mary, 11

Goodrich, Benjamin, 17, 28, 31
David, 17, 32
Ebenezer, 31
Elizur, 17
Hannah, 15, 17
Honor, 13
John, 17
Mary, 17
Rhoda, 17, 26
Sarah, 17
Zebulon, 27, 31
Zebulon, Jr., 32

Graham, Clara, 17

Graham, Hannah, 17
Hannah (Hunn), Mrs. John, 17
John, 17, 31
Love, 20
Mary, 17
Samuel, 17
Sarah, 17

Griswold, Josiah, 17
Mary, wife of Jonathan, 28

Guinea, [Negro], 25

H
Hayden, Pelatiah, 25

Holabud, Charles, 27. See also Hurlbut

Holebut, Charles, 28. See also Hurlbut

Holtom, Abigail, 31

Hooker, Daniel, 29
Elijah, 32

Howard, Edward, 26

Hunn, David, 17
Elisheba, 17
Enos, 17
Esther (Smith), Mrs. Enos, 17
Eunice, 17
Gideon, 17, 27, 30, 31, 32
Hannah, 17
Jemima, 18
Rebecca, 17
Rebecca, Mrs. Gideon, 17
Samuel, 28, 29
Thankful, 16

Hurlbut, Holabud, Holebut, Abigail, 23
Absalom, 18
Amos, 17, 31
Charles, 17, 27, 28, 31
Christopher, 31
Eleanor, (Ellener), 18
Eli, 30
Elias, 17, 31
Elizabeth, 14
Fitch, 18, 31
Hannah, 18
Jemima, 18
Jemima (Hunn), Mrs. Fitch, 18
Jerusha, 17

38

Lowrey, Mary, 19

Lusk, Abigail Belden, 20
  Abigail (Belden), Mrs. James, 20
  Elijah, 20
  Ethan, 26
  Hannah, 15
  James, 20, 31
  Jane, Mrs. John, 19, 27
  John, 19, 31
  Levi, 20
  Love (Graham), Mrs. James, 20
  Mary, 20

M

Marks, Abisha, 20
  Asahel, 20
  Bildad, 20
  Rhoda (Latimer), Mrs. Abisha, 20

Meekins, Rebecca, 13

Merrel, Mary, 31

Mills, Elizabeth, (Betsey), 20
  Jedidiah, 20
  Julia, 20
  Sarah, (Sally), 20
  Sarah (Andrus), Mrs. Jedidiah, 20

Mingo, [Negro], 25

Mitchell, Hannah (Warner), Mrs. James, 25
  James, 25, 32
  James, Jr., 25
  William, 25

Mitchelson, Mary, 12

Morris, ——, 20

Munsell, Hannah, 24

Mygatt, Zebulon, 20

N

Nott, Elizabeth, 24
  Tabitha, 18

P

Patterson, James, 29

Pegg, [Negro], 25

Pomp, [Negro], 25

Pratt, Hannah (Wolcott), Mrs. Samuel, 27
  Huldah, 27
  Lydia, 27
  Samuel, 27

Price, Abigail, 17
  Jerusha, 25

Prince, [Negro], 25

R

Richards, Janna, 20
  Joseph, 20, 31
  Joseph, Jr., 20
  Lucretia, 20, 30
  Lydia, Mrs. Samuel, 20
  Mary (Kelsey), Mrs. Joseph, 20
  Oliver, 20
  Pelatiah, 20, 30
  Samuel, 20
  Samuel, Dr., 31
  Selah, 20
  Seth, 20, 30
  Thomas, 20
  William, 20, 30

Robbins, Abigail, 21
  Hannah, 18
  Martin, 21
  Mary (Kellogg), Mrs. Unni, 20
  Prudence, 21
  Thomas, 28
  Unni, 20, 31
  Unni, Jr., 21
  Zebulon, Corporal, 28

Russell, David, 21
  Elizabeth, 18

S

Seymour, Abel, 21
  Abigail (Welles), Mrs. Ashbel, 26
  Ashbel, 21, 26, 31
  Ashbel, Jr., 26
  Bavil, 31
  David, 21
  Elias, 21, 31
  Elizabeth, 21
  Elizabeth (Wolcott), Mrs. Elias, 21
  Erastus, 26
  Eunice, 21
  George, 21
  Jerusha, 21

39

Seymour, Lois, 21
  Nancy, 21
  Thankful, 21
  Theodore, 21

Smith, Dorothy, 19
  Elizabeth (Kellogg), Mrs. Jedi-
    diah, 26
  Esther, 17
  Jedidiah, 26
  Luscinda, 21
  Obadiah, 27

Squire, Squier, John, 21, 31
  John, Jr., 21
  Lois, 21, 29
  Lucy, 21
  Rhoda, 21
  Rozetta, 21
  Rozetta (Blinn, Kirkham), Mrs.
    John, 21

Standish, Hannah, 32
  James, 32

Stedman, Elisha, 31

Steel, James, Jr., 31
  Joseph, 21
  Olive (Churchill), Mrs. Joseph,
    21
  Samuel, 32

Step, [Negro], 25

Stephens, Lois (Whaples), 11

Stoddard, Abigail, 22, 26
  Abigail (Atwood), Mrs. Eli, 22
  Anne, 22, 30
  Anne (Andrus), Mrs. Solomon,
    22
  Benjamin, 22
  Candace, 22
  Chloe, 21
  David, 22, 31
  Dinah (Fuller), Mrs. Enoch, 22
  Dorothy (Willard), Mrs. Elisha,
    21
  Eli, 22, 31
  Elisha, 21, 27, 30
  Elisha, Jr., 21
  Elizabeth, 30
  Enoch, 22, 31
  Esther, 30
  Eunice, 11
  Honor, 22

Stoddard, Jehiel, 22
  Jennet, 22
  Jesse, 22
  Jonathan, 22, 31
  Jonathan, Jr., 22
  Joseph, 22, 31
  Joseph, Jr., 22
  Levi, 22
  Mabel, 30
  Mary, 22
  Mary (Fuller), Mrs. Joseph, 22
  Melliscent, 16
  Olive, 22
  Percy, 22
  Rhoda, 22
  Roxalana, 22
  Sabara, 22
  Sabara (Andrus), Mrs. Jona-
    than, 22
  Samuel, 30
  Simeon, 21
  Solomon, 22, 31
  Sybil, 11
  Thomas, 28, 31
  Zebulon, 22, 28

T

Tryon, Aaron, 31

W

Warner, Daniel, 23
  Hannah, 25

Warren, Abraham, 28

Waters, Benjamin, 32

Weaver, Edward, 23
  Hannah, 23
  Mary, 23

Webster, David, 30
  Medad, 31
  Samuel, 31

Welles, Wells, Abigail, 23, 26
  Abigail (Burnham), Mrs. Rob-
    ert, 23
  Abigail (Hurlbut), Mrs. Robert,
    Jr., 23
  Absalom, 23
  Alma, 23
  Appleton, 23, 27, 30
  Austin, 24
  Beulah, 24
  Chester, 23

Wright, David, (Drummer), 28
  Elizabeth, 29
  Esther, 25
  Esther (Andrus), widow of
    Thomas, 25
  John, 25
  Josiah, 29
  Judah, 28

Wright, Lydia, 25
  Michael, 25
  Sarah, 25
  Thomas, 31

Y

Young, Steadman, 28

www.ingramcontent.com/pod-product-compliance
Lightning Source LLC
Chambersburg PA
CBHW052109270326
41931CB00012B/2943